THE DEAL

Tammy Golden

DEDICATION

This book is dedicated to my one and only son, Brandon James Golden-Taliferro. The love of my life, my inspiration, motivation, and will forever is my why. Happy Birthday!

CONTENTS

INTRODUCTION

I never thought I'd have this story to tell. I have actually been documenting and journaling my own personal crisis in which God revealed my purpose to me, but yet it involves so many components that I am still living through that it's just not time to tell my story yet. But what I am going to share is a portion of the series of events that forever changed my life.

A few days ago my one and only son took a deal on a case that he has been fighting for the last eight months. A case that could have cost him the rest of his life in jail and he is only twenty four. Last week while in court awaiting his second prelim hearing he was presented a deal. An offer to keep the case from going to trial, this case had been to trial once and because it wasn't in favor of the prosecution and we had a public defender willing to fight they dismissed the case before the jury was sworn in. This allows them to refile the case, continue to build their evidence and move the case to a more favorable court room.

We honestly didn't see it coming since they had never offered a deal. But once the new district attorney saw how eager my son wanted a speedy trial and based on the evidence (in which I will not disclose), they also ran the risk of losing if a jury had to hear this. So what happens when you don't have the resources to hire a good attorney? You get a public defender, whose only job is to play the middle man between the defendant and the prosecution to get the conviction with as little cost to the state as possible. They can save time and money while they play let's make a deal with the defendants lives. What happened to innocent until proven guilty?

I learned a lot those eight months in court. The most I had ever seen a courtroom was for some minor traffic tickets. I had a chance to witness the justice system at work and I can tell you it is not pretty and it sure as hell isn't fair. Deals are given out like an episode of Oprah's favorite things. You get a deal…. You get a deal… everybody gets a deal. Now I'm not saying these guys or even my own son are guilty, but they are given such exaggerated charges to get the arrest, with even stiffer penalties, that without a private attorney they are really left no option but to take the deal, and sadly a large number of these offenders are black males.

It's no secret that black men get higher penalties than other races. The time I have spent in the court room taught me a great deal about how the system works. It's the only place where I realized black lives mattered. It's the only place that they will freely let you in and do their best not to see them leave. I even witnessed a bailiff threaten to lock up everyone in the court room because a young man asked a family in the courtroom a question , the male member of the family refused to respond since the young man appeared as if there was an argument. It wasn't, he was just simply ignoring the young man who seemed mentally ill. The bailiff became aggressive asking did we have a problem. I thought to myself we? Then he asked us who wanted to go to jail? I turned my head the opposite way because this was pure foolishness. There were only four of us black in the court room awaiting our family members turn for their hearing. I wonder if the court room was white if he would have responded the same. Utter ridiculousness, it's not a place you want to visit if you don't have to. A white male kills nine people in a church and flees, upon his capture he is treated to a fast food meal. Did Sandra Bland ever find out why she was being arrested?

1 MY JOY

From the moment my son was born he was charming, entertaining, and had a very strong will. He was and is always a joy to be around. He has the ability to light up any room and if his presence irritated you then you're probably just an unhappy person that didn't like being around happy people. But no matter where he went he carried that gift with him. Being an only child he learned how to socialize quickly. He enjoyed being around people and knew how to command the attention of any audience. A smart kid, talented, and athletic his social skills would sometimes cause him to be distracted easily which would lead to phone calls home from a teacher saying, He's a great kid but he needs to settle down, no matter where I move him he talks." We never found the solution for that, it is who he is. No matter how much I would admonish him to control his talking an entertaining it was impossible. He's a natural and possesses a gift many would pay for. As a kid he had so much charisma, he'd spend time at my salon after school entertaining my clients. Outside of that like any kid he enjoyed basketball; football, video games, and pretty much mastered anything he put his mind to. His high school years became tougher. The social skills got the best of him so his school work began to go downhill. It didn't help that I moved to a community that began to have a negative influence on him. His interest began to change from sports to just hanging out and house parties. So as school declined I continued to find alternative programs just to get him through. He got approved for Job Corps. which I hope he would get his diploma and take a trade. He hated it and rushed his way through a simple skill, took the G.E.D. and left. Instead of taking advantage of the opportunities he wanted to get back to socializing. He was a very strong willed kid, I remember as he would learn to tie his shoes or buckle his belt, he only needed to watch you a few times, then from there he would not let you help him. And when he would get in trouble, he always manages to escape punishment.

I raised him on the west side of Los Angeles to keep him diverse. Like any parent I wanted a provided the best I could being a single parent and did my best for him not to experience the limiting lifestyle I grew up in. But no matter how hard I tried I couldn't prepare him for life as a black male. As a kid he never experienced racism that I can recall. But when he was about 10 years old I remember walking into a drug store in which we had just left a store and he was carrying my small bag. He ran ahead of me and entered the store and I was about 20 ft. behind him. The security guard saw him before he saw me and proceeded to follow my son around the store. I knew he was only running to the toy section. I watched him tailgate him around and once my son got to the toy section I asked the office could I help him. I took my sons hand as he was approaching him and the guard just turned around and went the other way. I surprised him and ruined whatever his intention was. At that moment I knew I would not always be around to defend such situations. It took sometime before my son would realize he was being treated different due to his skin color and larger body type, but by time he became a teenager he began to understand what it was like to be a black male in America.

After he left Job Corp he returned to his friends and gravitated back to the environment that was not conducive to his future. We went through periods of tough love, but by now he was 18 and if he didn't want to follow my rules it would frequently land him a one way ticket through the front door. It's hard for a young male trying to define his manhood but testing it on his mom is the wrong thing to do. Punishment never had an effect on him. If he wanted something bad enough no penalties could stop him. I always knew it would bite him in the butt one day.

[1]*"Legislators want to make it easy for prosecutors to get the conviction without having to go to trial," said Rachel Barkow, a professor of law at New York University who studies how prosecutors use their power. "And prosecutors who are starved for resources want to use that leverage. And so now everyone acts with the assumption that the case should end with a plea."*

"When you have that attitude," she said, "you penalize people who have the nerve to go to trial."

2 THE CALL

It was October last year that he happened to be at my home for the weekend. I became really ill and sharing with him that I was short of breathes. He later left and I began to feel really bad, I contacted him to let him know I needed to get to the hospital so when he returned I'd be ready. He called 911 since I had been complaining all day and they came, took me to emergency and he met us there. He stayed with me in the hospital helping me out and spent some time with me when I was released. As I began to feel better I, my usual motherly talk kicked in, what's your plans today son? Get a job… go to school… just do something. Like many young adults he was lost and didn't know what he wanted to do. Since I was recovering I didn't want to continue stressing myself by pushing him, something in my spirit told me to just pray for him. Pray he finds his purpose and that he remains safe. So I did and as I would see him walk in and out of my house I would just say a silent prayer.

A few weeks later I got the worst phone call a mother ever wants to hear. His girlfriend's mom called to tell me my son had been shot. I lost my breath and began to have a severe anxiety attack. I couldn't breathe and my heart was pounding, I couldn't talk and I was trying to pray at the same time. He was in surgery. I raced to my car and rushed to the hospital. Talk about a nightmare, as when I got to the hospital I met with one of the nurses who let me know that he was stable and they were doing vascular surgery to repair his arteries in his leg.

When he came out of surgery I went to see him and was greeted by two sheriffs that I assumed where wanting information about his shooting. They asked how he was doing and if he'd seen the person that shot him. He was in a lot of pain, they eventually left. The Dr. said it would be sometime before his leg would be stitched up since it was swollen and needed to completely drain before closing. So I and my family started routine visits to see him. He kept mentioning the sheriffs coming to question him but they never came while I was there.

A few weeks later his girlfriend called me one morning to say she couldn't find him at the hospital. I called and kept getting routed to the sheriff's dept. I told them my son had been in the hospital, gave them the name and they mentioned he was on a protective floor, and they would have an officer contact me. I asked could I come and see him like I do daily and they said no. Later an officer called asking a few to many questions. I asked if he was being held or protected. He said they were investigating a situation with little detail. I asked did my son need a lawyer, they said no. Meanwhile I can't see him and or talk to him but he is in the hospital still with his leg wide open about 8 inches on each side.

I made some phone calls and a friend referred an attorney who made some calls. The officers claimed they didn't have him in their custody but did say he was not free to leave. Now the nightmare worsens and I know it was only the grace of God that has kept me throughout the entire ordeal. Not only was I barely recovering from my own crisis but I had to also take on my son's situation. I asked God, is this going to help him find his purpose?

I finally got the call from a correctional institution; it was my son now at the medical ward, incarcerated. He sounded so distraught, I was devastated. He said mom they came in the room as soon as you left out the last time you saw me; in fact they were waiting for you to leave. He said they never moved him to a protective floor; they had an officer sit in the room with him interrogating him as well as tampering with his medical devices and prohibiting him from sleeping. They even got the Dr. to prematurely try to close

his leg before moving him to the jail hospital. To
make matters worse as soon as he came out of
surgery they put him in a van out in the air to
transport him with an open wound so that they
could get him booked within the time frame needed
to not have to let him go. His leg was not in
condition to close. Two days later he was back in
surgery getting it opened due to infection. The new
Dr. cleaned it, dressed it, and decided to keep him
on the wound vac for draining. Unfortunately he
couldn't get the sheriffs to follow his orders when it
came to his care. The machine was electronically
operated so whenever he was transported to court it
needs to stay plugged up. But because they didn't
care he would spend all day in holding at the court
house without the machine being plugged up so he
would return to the hospital in the same condition.
This was severely impeding his ability to heal. They
didn't care. My child was suffering so, not only was
he recovering from his injury, he was incarcerated,
and being treated unfairly. But I continued to pray
and ask God to take care of my son to touch the
heart of the caregivers to have mercy on my son
and put his care above his booking number, in
addition to calling the nurse station warning them if
my son loss his leg I would hold them all
responsible. I'd try my best not to cry on the phone,
I would just say son pray and trust God. But when I
would hang up my heart would drop to the floor.

This was unbelievable.

As a parent I use to say, if you ever go to jail don't call me. Well we all say things we don't mean right. I did. I had to learn a lot really fast. I was new to the prison system and the process. I have never visited a jail before or visited a loved one. I got my first visit while he was in the jail hospital. As the Sheriff escorted me down the cold halls it felt creepy. The sounds of chains and metal doors, ugh… but I was there to see my son so I had to become a big girl and go handle my business. Trying not cry I began my breathing exercise, heart pounding they sit me in a chair at steel screened gate, later they push a man out in wheel chair which was my son. The holes in the screen were so small you couldn't see anything but the silhouette. But you could hear the voice. We met for about 20 minutes, he said he was ok; his leg was doing better and assured me he was fine which he did frequently. He didn't want me to worry. It was too late for that. I had been worried most of his teen and adult life. I would have to continue to pray God's will be done in this situation.

Once his leg was pretty stable then they moved him to Twin Towers Treatment Center. The Dr. gave them strict instructions for moving his equipment. But no, they neglect all orders and my son ends up two days in intake, no food or meds nor was he plugged up on his machine, the leg began swelling and draining and bleeding in the lobby and he couldn't get any help. When he finally got through processing, he was so sick that he had to be rushed back to the hospital. He said the Dr. saw him and wondered why he was back. He explained what happened and the Dr. made a phone call to the treatment center to blast them for putting my son's health at risk which could cause them all serious problems. They stabilized him and sent him back to Twin Towers.

He'd spend the next six months advocating for his care and even learned how to change and dress his wound himself, the nursed didn't want to be bothered often so they would leave him the wound kit and he would change it his self.

[2] *The report, "Criminal: How Lockup Quotas and 'Low-Crime Taxes' Guarantee Profits for Private Prison Corporations," documents the contracts exchanged between private prison companies and state and local governments that either guarantee prison occupancy rates (essentially creating inmate lockup quotas) or force taxpayers to pay for empty beds if the prison population decreases due to lower crime rates or other factors (essentially creating low-crime taxes).*
Some of these contracts require 90 to 100 percent prison occupancy.
In a letter to 48 state governors in 2012, the largest for-profit private prison company in the US, Corrections Corporation of America (CCA), offered to buy up and operate public state prisons. In exchange, states would have to sign a 20-year contract guaranteeing a 90 percent occupancy rate throughout the term.

3 HELD OVER

The next six months would also be spent going back and forth to court only to get the case extended for another 14 to 28 days. The charges he was facing were serious, but the evidence didn't quite add up. All of these extensions were simply to buy time to keep fishing for evidence.

Once he was moved to the treatment center things got a little lighter for him as his leg began to heal. We would talk often and I would visit as often as I could. The first visit to Twin Towers wasn't as hard as I expected. I had heard a lot of storied but heck I was now living a story. You learn a lot and fast. After you get checked in you get directed where to go to visit the inmate. The long walk down the hall, at least it seemed long was so full of concrete and iron gates. The ceiling seemed to get lower the further back you went. I would practice my breathing and mentally prepare to see him. He looked better and healthy and was still in a wheel chair, said his leg was healing fine. We'd make small talk laugh and keep a positive conversation and I'd remind him to pray. It's funny how life can slow us down and reconnect us with the Divine. He was reading more and sharing with me from his readings. He also was learning to meditate. The hardest part of the visits were was always at the end when the guard would come and take him back and all you could do was touch the glass and say bye.

Those were the tears harder to control. I now realize that every person that was exiting the visiting area would be shedding the same tear.

We couldn't retain and attorney so we opted for a public defender and to leave the rest up to God. I had just returned to work and was rebuilding my business. I suggest every parent set aside money for a retainer, you never know if you might need it, and it's easier to fight a case in prelim with an attorney than during a trial. Our public defender was actually interested in defending the case and saw the same issues in the testimonies that we did. Not once was there mention of a deal.

In and out of court, what I called dancing with the devil I witnessed so many of these men young and old had very little support for them if any on court day. I hated going but I was not going to let my son fight this alone. Once he was arrested how soon learned that family and friends come a dime a dozen and that they could even be bought for a penny on a dollar. When he was shot friends came around.

When he was arrested they disappeared.
Our family dynamics is selectively supportive and
extremely judgmental so I learned to limit my
conversations because the opinions of a few were
not my concern and since everyone has one I let
them enjoy it. What my son and many in that
position need is unconditional love. When the
world is against you the last thing you need is
friends or family that is just nosey and
unsupportive. I've learned the less they know the
less they could tell or gossip about and the less hear
say would return to me.
This was and is me and my son's journey. He also
had his girlfriend as support. My son was no angel
and has made mistakes, but who hasn't. Yes I'd
wish he had listened to the much advice and
counsel he had received from me, family, and other
leaders in his life but he is a strong willed child and
many things he has had to learn from experience.
But when people start giving judgmental advice you
really steer clear. I even was told to tell him to tell
his lawyer the truth, based on what evidence did
they think he was lying, and this is why I avoid
ignorant people to prevent myself from being
disrespectful to a family member. So I minimized
my updates. No one will love your child like you do.
So it was me and him.
As his leg got better they were preparing to move
him to Men's Central Jail into the general

population, I can tell he was nervous about it. Now he was going to be in a more aggressive population. The treatment center was for the mental ill, sick, and handicapped inmates. I arranged a visit at that location, it was much different. If the looks of the visitors were a reflection on the inmates I knew it must have been a wild bunch. Sure enough once I was cleared to visit him and went to the window where we would meet a rowdy bunch of inmates came out to the visiting tank. My prayer was Lord let my son not make any new friends in here and become accustomed to this environment.

[3]*After emancipation, a loophole in the 13th Amendment retained legal slavery for those who'd been duly convicted of a crime. In 1867, Texas began leasing out its convicts to labor for private companies, and former plantations across the state were transformed into prison farms. The vast majority of the men and women who toiled on them were African-Americans, either the children of slaves or former slaves themselves, who came from states like Arkansas and Louisiana as well as from across Texas... "How are you going to now take almost 5 million human beings who were previously in bondage, who have no interest whatsoever in working on plantations where they were enslaved, and basically force [them] into involuntary servitude?" McGhee asked. "How are you going to compel them to labor for you? This is how it was done."*

Convict leasing's popularity in Texas caught on gradually over the mid-to-late 19th century, but became a well-established practice for the state by the 1890s, being utilized to construct the state capital, operate the Ellis Plantation's newly-built sugar mill, and perform the back-breaking labor of cultivating its surrounding cane fields. The practice was greatly facilitated by the "Black Codes," a series of openly racist laws passed by southern states in the years after the Civil War, which ensnared free African-Americans into involuntary servitude for crimes like vagrancy. Texas Slave Descendent Society founder Reginald Moore, himself a former Texas Department of Corrections employee at the Jester Unit in Richmond, said once a black person became entangled in the convict labor leasing system, the Black Codes – also known as the "Pig Law" – made it virtually impossible to escape.

"They would re-incarcerate you [after being released], and would be able to get the free labor by saying you were just a vagrant that didn't have a job and was fresh out [of jail]," Moore said. "That would be reason to enslave you again, to put you in the system. With the Pig Law, if you got caught stealing a pig, you got 15 years. The pig could have been a wild, feral hog."

4 DEAL OR NO DEAL

We finally got a court date. The prosecution had made no offer and neither had we. His public defender had put together a defense that he thought could create reasonable doubt and some of the evidence was questionable. I had the pleasure of shopping for an outfit for my son to wear in court. While many were preparing for their kids to graduate from college I was preparing for my son to go on trial for a case that could cause him to spend the rest of his life in jail. The jury pool was in place and we were ready to dance. I was nervous and anxious and once again mustering up the strength to be strong for my son. Once again the witnesses had not appeared and jury was being questioned by the judge. The jury from another case had notified the judge they were ready to give their verdict, so they dismissed us all to return the next day.

I chose to work and his girlfriend went and was texting me what was going on. I wanted to be there for opening statements so I chose to finish my clients during jury selection. I got a text from her saying that the jury was sent home and she didn't know why. The public defender called and said the case had been dismissed, the witnesses were still missing and that they would refile the case the next day, meaning he stayed in custody. Apparently if you dismiss before the jurors are sworn in you can refile the case, if you dismiss after they are sworn in it becomes double jeopardy. Knowing that the case was nothing without the witness and that our public defender was actually putting up a fight they ran a huge risk in losing. So they dismissed and refiled in the original court house which moved the case to a more favorable location for them.

He was upset. He was appointed a new Public Defender who rarely had time or cared to discuss his case. At the arraignment my son exercised his right to a speedy trial which was denied. The new prosecution claimed they needed more time to get the witnesses in, but that also let her know that my son was wanting to go to trial and based on the evidence I know of if reasonable doubt could be created they could lose this case. They eventually bought themselves about six weeks of time before the preliminary hearing. We came prepared for a hearing and a trial date to be set. The public defender hadn't discussed his defense with my son.

We arrived and when the public defender walked in I heard him mention a possible offer from the

D.A., I thought my son told him no deals, so why was he was initiating this without consulting with my son. He went back to talk to my son and had been with him for a while. When he came out he asked to speak to me, we walked outside and he told me my son was interested in taking a deal. My heart started racing. This came as a big surprise. Tears started flowing and had to take a moment and gather myself. He said my son wanted to talk with me first. I agreed, the court broke for lunch and he called me. He said, "Well Momma this is it… Imma have to take the deal. This man is not fighting for me and if we lose I won't be coming home and I want to come home." I was devastated, he said, "even with the discrepancies in the testimonies that the public defender didn't care to entertain he felt there was one witness he didn't stand a chance defending." My son sounded pretty calm but I knew he was making the best decision for his future. I was crying uncontrollably. He said mom, "I'm sorry, I know you didn't raise me this way and I hate to hear you cry, but without anyone fighting for me I have no choice." I agreed and told him I didn't think I could return to the court room but to call me when he returned to the jail. Fate would have it that my cell phone died and I couldn't call my ride so I ended up being there when they returned from lunch. I saw the public defender go inside and at that moment I decided well I'm here, and if my son is going to take the deal he deserves my support until the end. I was silently deep breathing to control my anxiety, dried up my tears and went inside. They called his case and the bailiff brought him in. His head was held high, shoulders back and pleaded no contest to the charges. He answered the judge with no hesitation and agreed to the terms of the sentence. Honestly I have never been more proud in my life. I witnessed my son become a man. The first time he entered that courtroom eight months ago he had loss so much weight from stress and lack of food he looked like a teenager, this day he was much stockier from lifting weights and was a man. When he turned to go back inside he looked at me and said I love you. I nodded and left the court room. It was done. Just that quick all the anxiety and stress was done. Part of me felt relieved, the other part was still devastated. Of course my phone was charged and I called my uber and went to work.

Later that night he called me, when I answered he said, "Momma I'm coming home"! I asked him how he felt, he said he felt good. He felt freer; he felt that he could accept the sentence if that was his only route home. I told him I was proud of him. He asked why? I said for the first time I seen you face the consequences of your actions, not that you were guilty of the crime but your associations and poor choices got you in this situation. He said, "Mom I have been able to get out of every situation I have been in, but this is one I couldn't." I said, "That's ok I believe God is still in control, and that your purpose is being discovered during this process and somehow this situation is actually saving your life." He agreed that he needed to slow down and focus and is just ready to get his exit date and serve his time. He kept saying, "Momma I'm coming home." He was getting a lot of advice from inmates so he was preparing to be moved to a state facility and make the most he can of the situation. I encouraged him to explore his options in the different trades they have available. If you are going to spend the next 5-6 years there you might as well make it count. He agreed. He sound in good spirits and that's the best I can hope for.

This experience has made us so much stronger and as painful as it has been it definitely developed some new prayer and faith muscles for us both. In the beginning I didn't know how I would get through it, but I stayed in prayer and affirming God's will be done and that he continue to guide my son and protect him while revealing his will for his life. Now he has time to hear and be ready to live his best life yet once he returns home.

TAMMY GOLDEN

5 OVERVIEW

One thing I know for sure is the system isn't fair. Are their some people there that deserve to be there, I'm sure. but there appears to be far more there simply because they cannot afford a lawyer to fight for them in a trial. How can someone facing life get handed a few years if he gives up his right to a fair trial? That's a slap in the face to the victim of the crime. I think it's the prosecutors way of getting the conviction by any means necessary and definitely punishing the defendant for trying to fight for their freedom. They do have the right to be defended but it appears only if you can afford an attorney willing to fight for you. So it makes sense, all the research I have done proves that black lives matter in jail. Why? Free labor. I began to realize, this country was built the American way, off of free labor. As a business owner I know how hard it is to pay fair wages an all the taxes associated with it. You see companies taking their production overseas to save cost. Which explains why sitting and listening to deals being made behind the defendants back. My son like many young men there was just bamboozled with an offer. They know their plan before they even walk in the court room. To sit there and listen to them toss numbers around on someone's life as if their life didn't matter, nor did the truth. They just appeared to need a number, a number a defendant was willing to give for his freedom, not for the crime but for his ticket home. No one wanted to know if they are guilty, they just need them to take the deal so that they can ensure a number of head counts meet the necessary criteria and increase their chances of returning to the system once they become criminalized in the system. I pray may son focuses on coming home. His personality is very adaptive and his social skills always make him popular, but I pray it's not at the cost of his future.

[4]*To demonstrate how difficult involvement in prison industries and the use of inmate labor is to identify, we'll begin with an investment firm involved in many of our 401(k) and retirement accounts.*

Fidelity Investments (Fidelity). This "financial investment" corporation is involved in holding the retirement and 401(k) accounts of millions of Americans. Many of the largest companies in our country offer Fidelity Investments as the sole source of retirement investing for their employees.

Fidelity was previously identified as a funder of the American Legislative Exchange Council (ALEC) in an earlir Insourcing blog. ALEC is deeply invested in supporting Corrections Corporation of American (CCA) and Geo Group (Geo) – that are both corporate members of ALEC. ALEC has willingly accepted responsibility for enactment of laws authorizing and increasing the use of inmates in manufacturing of products as well as the housing of those inmates by private corporations such as CCA and Geo.

Unfortunately if your retirement savings, 401(K) or other investments are held by Fidelity, chances are some of your money is invested by Fidelity in either the use of prison labor or in other operations related to the prison industrial complex (PIC).

I purposely mentioned McDonald's in the intro because though they are not "directly" using inmate labor in their food service operations, they are dependent upon the use of inmate labor to reduce costs associated with those operations. The way they do this is by contracting to purchase their uniforms and some of the plastic utensils provided to customers from a company using inmate labor to make those uniforms and utensils. The uniforms are made by Oregon Inmates. Wendy's has also been identified as relying upon prison labor to reduce their cost of operations – and they fund ALEC.

Two other U.S. companies relying upon prison labor for products sold in their stores are K-Mart and J.C. Penny. Both sell Jeans made by inmates in Tennessee prisons. The same prison in Tennessee provides labor for Eddie Bauer's wooden rocking horses. There are other products we would not associate with prison made products: dentures, partials, eye glasses, processed foods such as beef, chicken and pork patties sold to and served in our schools, grocery stores and hospitals. I don't know about you but putting dentures made in prison in my mouth just somehow causes me concern...just as buying a box of breaded chicken patties and fixing them for my family does.

What about services such as Insurance? Banking? Utilities – gas, oil, electricity? Prescription drugs? Are all of these services or commodities tied to prison labor and the PIC? Unfortunately, yes. many insurance companies are tied to ALEC...as are corporations involving utilities provided to you in your city or town. To name just a few brand names you'll recognize that are invested in prison labor or PIC through ALEC are:

BANKS*: American General Financial Group, American Express Company, Bank of America, Community Financial Services Corporation, Credit Card Coalition, Credit Union National Association, Inc., Fidelity Investments, Harris Trust & Savings Bank, Household International, LaSalle National Bank, J.P. Morgan & Company, Non-Bank Funds Transmitters Group*

ENERGY PRODUCERS/OIL: *American Petroleum Institute, Amoco Corporation, ARCO, BP America, Inc., Caltex Petroleum, Chevron Corporation, ExxonMobil Corporation, Mobil Oil Corporation, Phillips Petroleum Company.*

ENERGY PRODUCERS/UTILITIES: *American Electric Power Association, American Gas Association, Center for Energy and Economic Development, Commonwealth Edison Company, Consolidated Edison Company of New York, Inc., Edison Electric Institute, Independent Power Producers of New York, Koch Industries, Inc., Mid-American Energy Company, Natural Gas Supply Association, PG&E Corporation/PG&E National Energy Group, U.S. Generating Company.*

INSURANCE: *Alliance of American Insurers, Allstate Insurance Company, American Council of Life Insurance, American Insurance Association, Blue Cross and Blue Shield Corporation, Coalition for Asbestos Justice, (This organization was formed in October 2000 to explore new judicial approaches to asbestos litigation." Its members include ACE-USA, Chubb & Son, CNA service mark companies, Fireman's Fund Insurance Company, Hartford Financial Services Group, Inc., Kemper Insurance Companies, Liberty Mutual Insurance Group, and St. Paul Fire and Marine Insurance Company. Counsel to the coalition is Victor E. Schwartz of the law firm of Crowell & Moring in Washington, D.C., a longtime ALEC ally.)*
Fortis Health, GEICO, Golden Rule Insurance Company, Guarantee Trust Life Insurance, MEGA Life and Health Insurance Company, National Association of Independent Insurers, Nationwide Insurance/National Financial, State Farm Insurance Companies, Wausau Insurance Companies, Zurich Insurance.

PHARMACEUTICALS: *Abbott Laboratories, Aventis Pharmaceuticals, Inc., Bayer Corporation, Eli Lilly & Company, GlaxoSmithKline, Glaxo Wellcome, Inc., Hoffman-LaRoche, Inc., Merck & Company, Inc., Pfizer, Inc., Pharmaceutical Research and Manufacturers of*
America (PhRMA), Pharmacia Corporation, Rhone-Poulenc Rorer, Inc., Schering-Plough Corporation, Smith, Kline & French, WYETH, a division of American Home Products Corporation.

MANUFACTURING:*American Plastics Council, Archer Daniels*

Midland Corporation, AutoZone, Inc. (aftermarket automotive parts), Cargill, Inc., Caterpillar, Inc., Chlorine Chemistry Council, Deere & Company, Fruit of the Loom, Grocery Manufacturers of America, Inland Steel Industries, Inc., International Game Technology, International Paper, Johnson & Johnson, Keystone Automotive Industries, Motorola, Inc., Procter & Gamble, Sara Lee Corporation.

TELECOMMUNICATIONS: AT&T, Ameritech, BellSouth Telecommunications, Inc., GTE Corporation, MCI, National Cable and Telecommunications Association, SBC Communications, Inc., Sprint, UST Public Affairs, Inc., Verizon Communications, Inc.

TRANSPORTATION: Air Transport Association of America, American Trucking Association, The Boeing Company, United Airlines, United Parcel Service (UPS).

OTHER U.S. COMPANIES: Amway Corporation, Cabot Sedgewick, Cendant Corporation, Corrections Corporation of America, Dresser Industries, Federated Department Stores, International Gold Corporation, Mary Kay Cosmetics, Microsoft Corporation, Newmont Mining Corporation, Quaker Oats, Sears, Roebuck & Company, Service Corporation International, Taxpayers Network, Inc., Turner Construction, Wal-Mart Stores, Inc.

ORGANIZATIONS/ASSOCIATIONS: Adolph Coors Foundation, Ameritech Foundation, Bell & Howell Foundation, Carthage Foundation, Charles G. Koch Charitable Foundation, ELW Foundation, Grocery Manufacturers of America, Heartland Institute of Chicago, The Heritage Foundation, Iowans for Tax Relief, Lynde and Harry Bradley Foundation of Milwaukee, National Pork Producers Association, National Rifle Association, Olin Foundation, Roe Foundation, Scaiffe Foundation, Shell Oil Company Foundation, Smith Richardson Foundation, Steel Recycling Institute, Tax Education Support Organization, Texas Educational Foundation, UPS Foundation.

5 LAST CALL

Well tonight he called, said he is packing his things head to the county facility to prepare to head to a state facility to serve his time. He sounded in good as spirit as he or anyone could be. He was always an adaptable child and always made the best of most situations he was faced with. When he sounds okay then I'm okay. Told me he loved me and he would contact me if he had chance before he gets on the bus but if not he has a letter prepared to drop in the mail as soon as he touches down to contact me. He won't be able to call for a while so we will have to write.

As I sit and look at his picture my eyes fill with tears. This hurts so bad. If I had to describe what it feels like I couldn't. This tops the pain of losing my best friend earlier this year and I wasn't prepared for that either. Every mother's instinct is to protect their child at all cost, I feel so helpless because I can't save him. God give me strength. My life will never be the same until my son returns.

You can only raise a child a guide their path, some will follow, some will explore a different path.

Ultimately they will make their own choices that may affect you both.
I can't do the time for him, this is his time to journey into the school of life. He now has to vouch for his self and make decisions that he can live with like the ones that got him there. Unfortunately these kids will never get the right to the fair trial the law speaks of because the deal gets the state a win by default. Even the victims have no say in the offer because it's truly not about the alleged crime. His time is deeply tied to a system that needs to institutionalizes these young men and to increase their chances of return to it. You can either learn from it or learn to like it. I pray my son learns from it and use his time wisely to discover his purpose and prepare to rebuild his life a few years from now.

Final Call

Friday my son called to let me know they were moving him to Men's Central to first then he would be taken to the State Prison from there. He said he would probably be moved Sunday night but would call as soon as they call his name to prepare to leave. Intake for State Prison is 45-90 days so it could be awhile before we are able to speak again.

I got a call Sunday evening and he shared that since Monday was a holiday they may not move him until Monday night or Tuesday morning. About two hours later he called again. This time he said, "Okay Mom, they just called my name, I'm out… I love you, take care of yourself and will talk to you soon." I replied, "I love you, be safe, and don't forget to pray." He said, "Ok, I'm just ready to get this over with and come home."

He sounded really good. When I say good I mean happy to moving forward to get through the next couple of years. I thought I would cry when he called to say goodbye, but him being in good spirits lifts my spirits. So if he can live with it the best he can, so can I.

PROLOGUE

Ten months ago I prayed to God to reveal my sons purpose to him so that he could find his path. Today I still believe that this journey is his path to finding his purpose.

Your purpose is so important. When you begin to pursue the path that God provides to your purpose you then have a reason. A reason to make better and smarter choices. Your purpose must be greater than anything that could distract you and cause you to miss your destiny.

I believe many of the men and women incarcerated either have never discovered or loss focus of their purpose, their calling and God's will in their life. When you know your purpose you must become conscious of the choices you make. Who you choose to associate with, spend time with, do business with, and even in a relationship with. You must also manage your emotions and thoughts and control the desire to get even or be right.

One must think before acting or reacting, what are the consequences of my action? What could this cost me? Could I lose my family, loved ones, or even my life? Most of all how much valuable time will I lose? Time is irreplaceable, you can replace money but never time.

Trust I have had thoughts play out in my head of reacting to people, even wondering where did the witness that planned to testify live? Yes my honest thought, but not a crime. I also had to think what would it cost me. I know my purpose is bigger than any prison and nothing or nobody is worth the crime or the time.

The day you discover your purpose is the day you begin living.

A special thank you to those that supported us in prayers and monetary support.

Footnotes
1
 August 2015
http://www.nytimes.com/2011/09/26/us/tough-sentences-help-prosecutors-push-for-plea-bargains.html?_r=2

2
August 2015
http://www.alternet.org/civil-liberties/6-shocking-revelations-about-how-private-prisons-make-their-money

3
August 2015
http://www.yourhoustonnews.com/sugar_land/news/ghosts-of-sugar-land/article_b41323b9-cd30-584f-8a4a-1805c9274a02.html

4
September 2015